AF269735

FIREFIGHTERS

A First Look

PERCY LEED

GRL Consultant, Diane Craig, Certified Literacy Specialist

Lerner Publications ◆ Minneapolis

Educator Toolbox

Reading books is a great way for kids to express what they're interested in. Before reading this title, ask the reader these questions:

What do you think this book is about? Look at the cover for clues.

What do you already know about firefighters?

What do you want to learn about firefighters?

Let's Read Together

Encourage the reader to use the pictures to understand the text.

Point out when the reader successfully sounds out a word.

Praise the reader for recognizing sight words such as *in* and *us*.

TABLE OF CONTENTS

Firefighters

Firefighters help keep us safe from fires.

5

Firefighters put
out fires.
They act fast!

Why must firefighters
act fast?

What do you wear
to keep you safe?

8

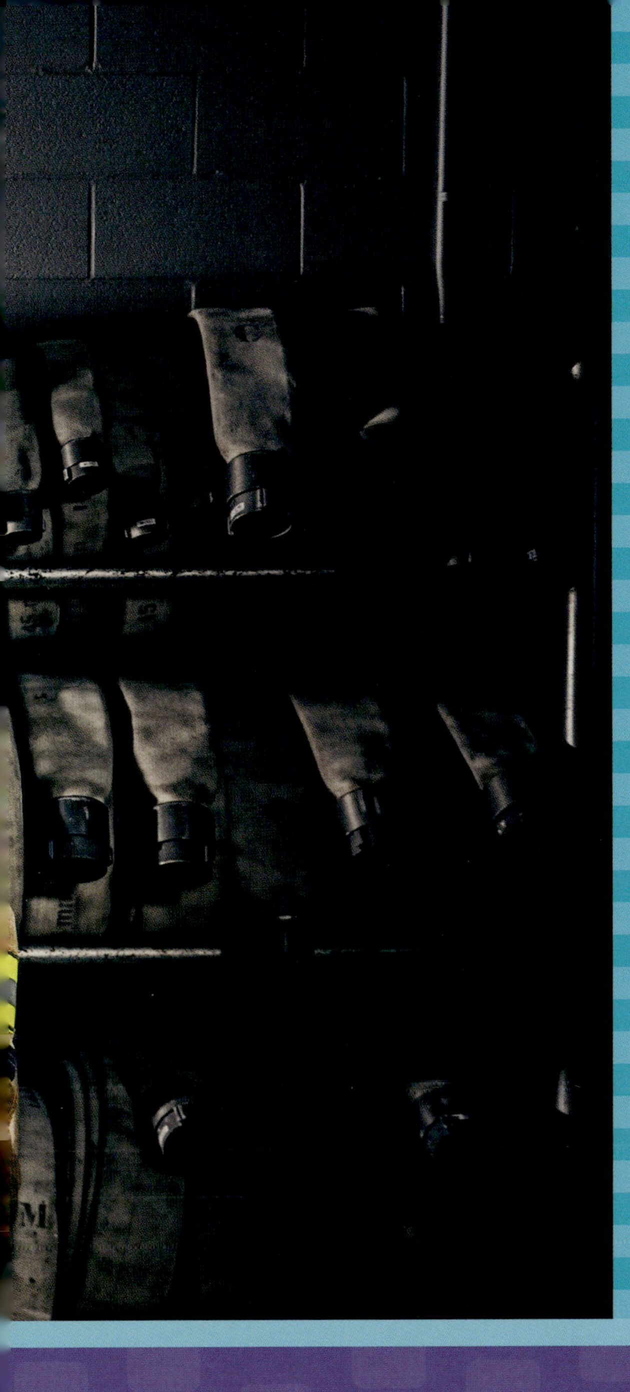

Firefighters wear clothes that keep them safe.

Firefighters drive
a fire truck.
It makes loud
sounds.

Why do fire trucks
make loud sounds?

11

Firefighters use a hose.
The water puts the
fire out.

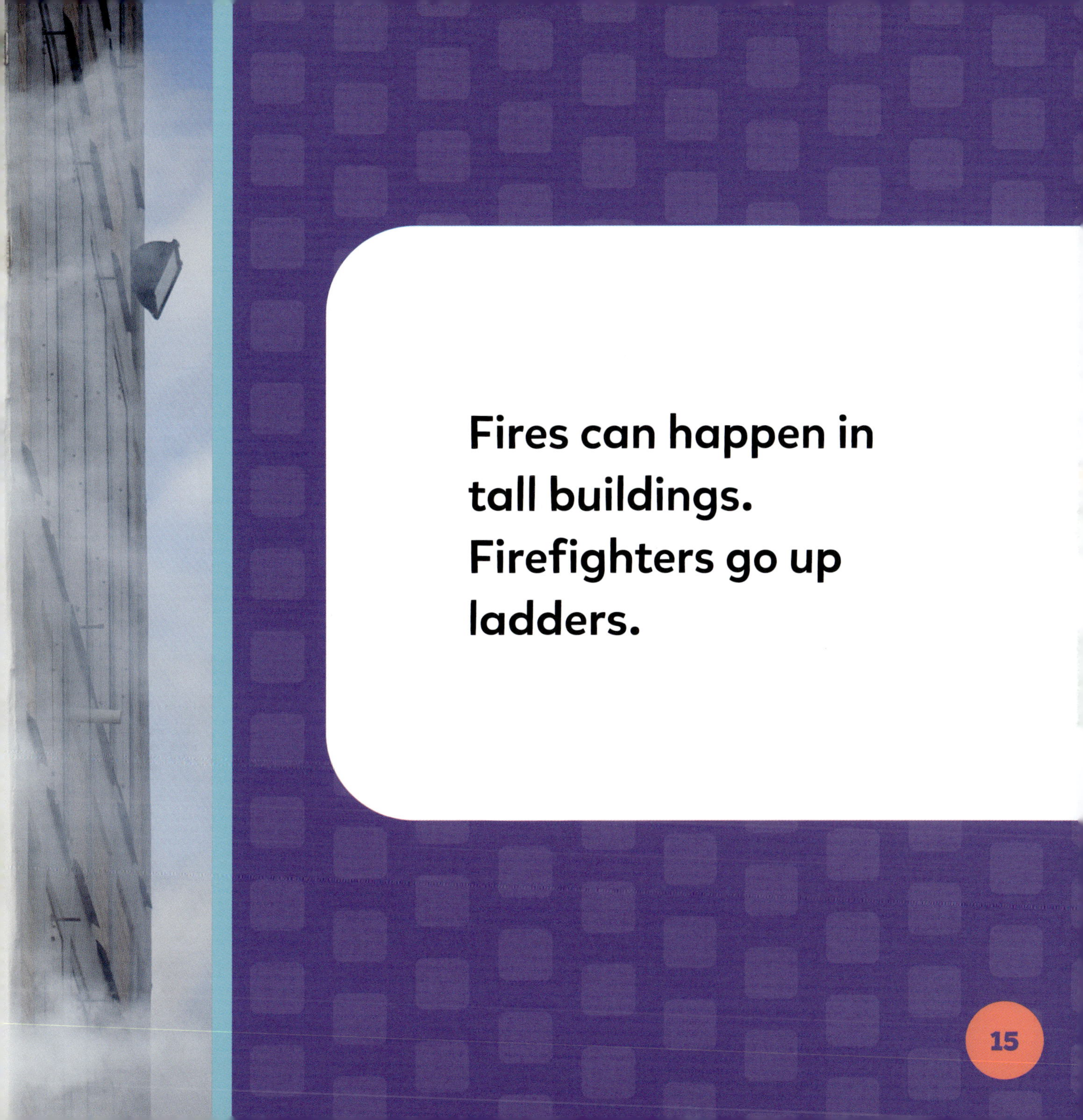

Fires can happen in
tall buildings.
Firefighters go up
ladders.

Sometimes firefighters
go into buildings that
are on fire.
They look for people.

Firefighters teach us about fire safety.

They teach us to have a
plan in case of a fire.

Firefighters work hard to keep us safe!

You Connect!

What is something you like about firefighters?

How can a firefighter help you?

Would you like to be a firefighter when you grow up?

Social and Emotional Snapshot

Student voice is crucial to building reader confidence. Ask the reader:

What is your favorite part of this book?

What is something you learned from this book?

Did this book remind you of any community helpers you've met?

Photo Glossary

Learn More

Boothroyd, Jennifer. *All about Firefighters*. Minneapolis: Lerner Publications, 2021.

Driscoll, Laura. *I Want to Be a Firefighter*. New York: Harper, 2022.

Leed, Percy. *Fire Trucks: A First Look*. Minneapolis: Lerner Publications, 2024.

Index

Photo Acknowledgments

The images in this book are used with the permission of: © LPETTET/iStockphoto, pp. 4–5; © JohnnyH5/iStockphoto, pp. 6–7; © Firefighter Montreal/Adobe Stock, pp. 8–9; © Jenny Thompson/Adobe Stock, pp. 10–11, 23 (top right); © xavierarnau/iStockphoto, pp. 12–13; © domonite/Adobe Stock, pp. 13, 23 (bottom left); © ollo/iStockphoto, pp. 14–15, 23 (top left, bottom right); © TatianaMironenko/iStockphoto, pp. 16–17; © Wavebreakmedia/iStockphoto, p. 18; © Hero Images/iStockphoto, p. 19; © VAKSMANV/Adobe Stock, p. 20.

Cover Photograph: © kali9/iStockphoto

Design Elements: © Mighty Media, Inc.

Lerner Publications Company
An imprint of Lerner Publishing Group, Inc.
241 First Avenue North
Minneapolis, MN 55401 USA

For reading levels and more information, look up this title at www.lernerbooks.com.

Main body text set in Mikado a Medium.
Typeface provided by Hannes von Doehren.

Library of Congress Cataloging-in-Publication Data

Names: Leed, Percy, 1968– author.
Title: Firefighters : a first look / Percy Leed.
Description: Minneapolis, MN : Lerner Publications, [2025] | Series: Read about community helpers | Includes bibliographical references and index. | Audience: Ages 5–8 | Audience: Grades K–1 | Summary: "Firefighters have very important jobs; they risk their lives to help us stay safe. With full-color photographs and engaging text, young readers can fight fires right alongside these heroic community helpers"– Provided by publisher.
Identifiers: LCCN 2023035532 (print) | LCCN 2023035533 (ebook) | ISBN 9798765626412 (library binding) | ISBN 9798765629536 (paperback) | ISBN 9798765636800 (epub)
Subjects: LCSH: Fire fighters–Juvenile literature. | Fire extinction–Juvenile literature.
Classification: LCC TH9148 .L38 2025 (print) | LCC TH9148 (ebook) | DDC 363.37092–dc23/eng/20230809

LC record available at https://lccn.loc.gov/2023035532
LC ebook record available at https://lccn.loc.gov/2023035533

Manufactured in the United States of America
1 – CG – 7/15/24